Advanced Patterns and Doodles
Adult Coloring Book

By Lilt Kids Coloring Books

D1418266

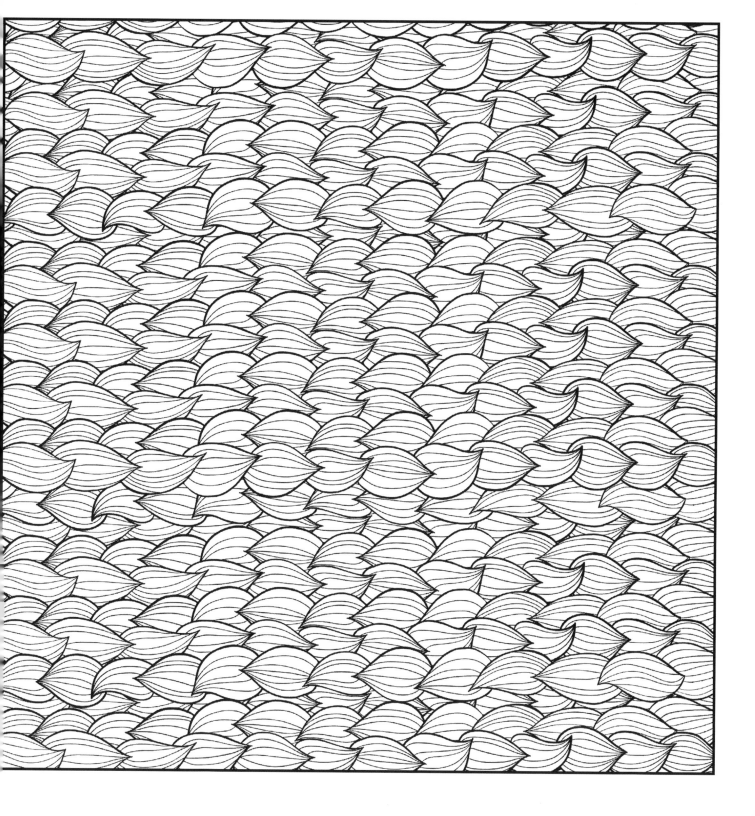

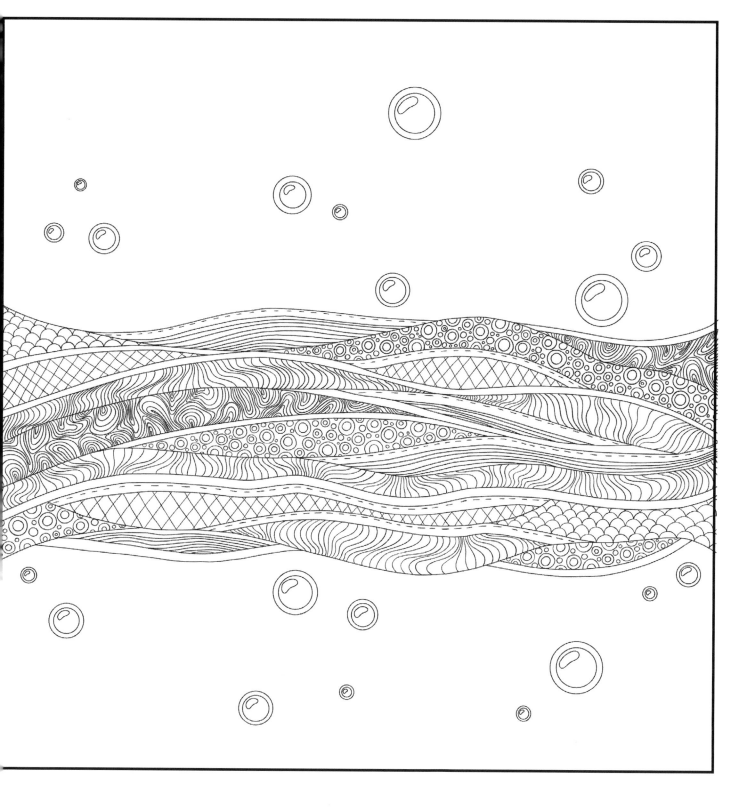

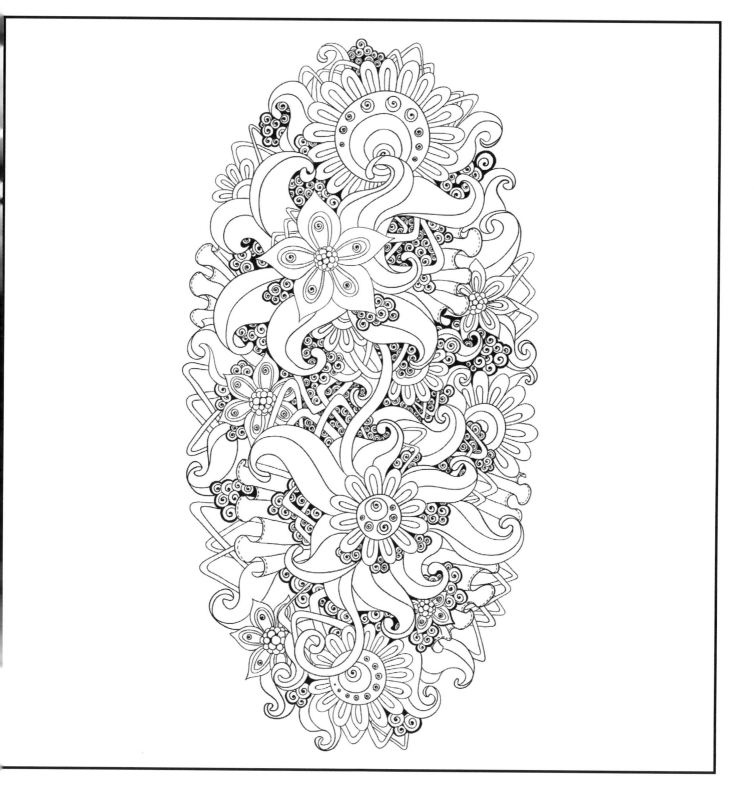

___

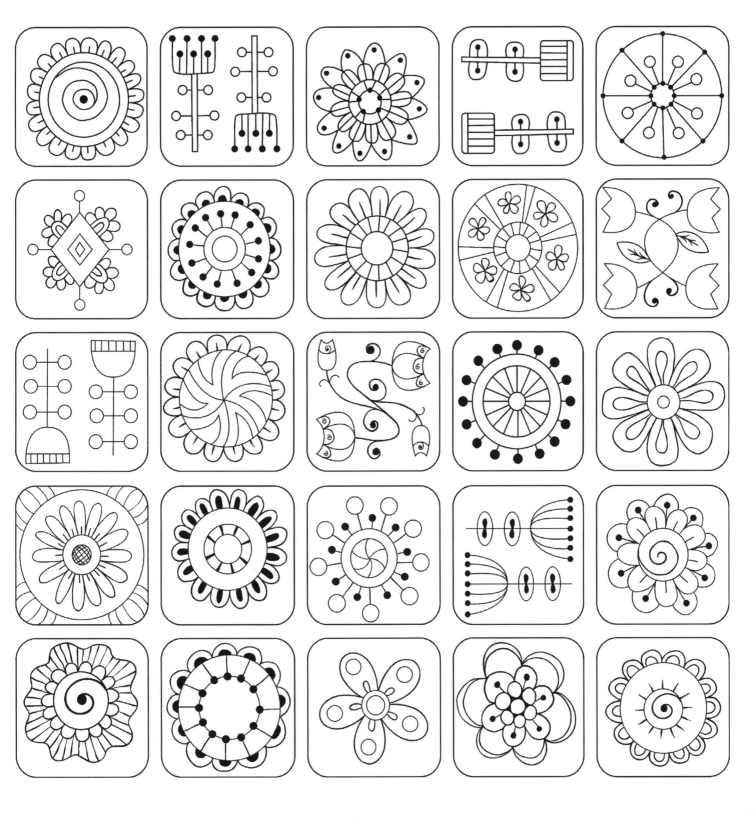

Did You Know?

We always give away the kindle version of a book
when it is first published.

Don't miss out!

Go to LiltKids.com to follow us on social media or
join our email list to learn about new, free books.

This coloring book comes with a free printable pdf version - so you can print another one when the kids are done with this one!

Go to

Liltkids.com/advanced-patterns

to download it.

Made in the USA
San Bernardino, CA
20 September 2014